...spected writer and editor
...author of many picture books
...millian) and *The Nightspinners*
...e commissioning editor for
...raction, the Eden Project.
...nces Lincoln are *Hair, Bicycles*
...Around the World series.

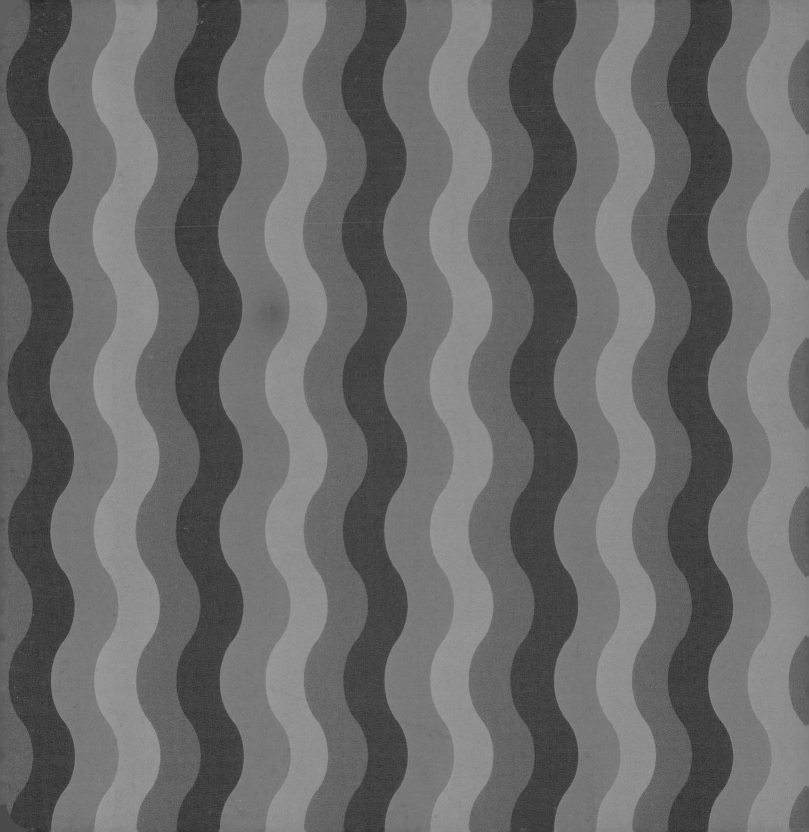

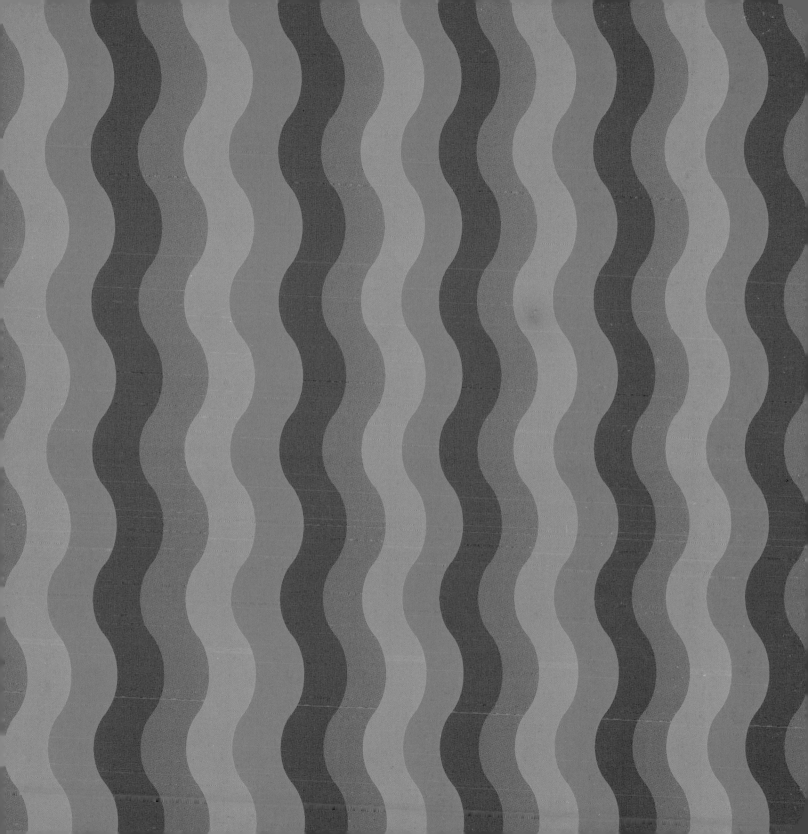

For Ella and Bella

Oxfam would like to acknowledge, with thanks, the following photographers:
Annie Bungeroth (pages 5 and 24–25), Howard Davies (pages 16–17), Richard Davis (pages 14–15),
Tim Dirven (pages 18–19), Julio Etchart (pages 8–9), Mark Henley (pages 12–13),
Crispin Hughes (pages 6–7 and back cover), Shailan Parker (pages 20–21 and cover),
Caroline Penn (pages 10–11) and Karen Robinson (pages 22–23) and Ami Vitale (pages 26-27).

First published in Great Britain in 2006 by
Frances Lincoln Children's Books, 4 Torriano Mews,
Torriano Avenue, London NW5 2RZ

www.franceslincoln.com

First paperback edition 2006

British Library Cataloguing in Publication Data available on request

ISBN 10: 1-84507-556-0
ISBN 13: 978-1-84507-556-9

Printed in China

3 5 7 9 8 6 4

Oxfam GB will receive a 4% royalty for each copy of this book sold in the UK.

Home

Kate Petty

FRANCES LINCOLN CHILDREN'S BOOKS
in association with

 **Oxfam**

Aluka lives in Uganda. There is a thick wall of sticks all around his homestead. He lives there with all his relatives.

I have to crouch down to get in!

This is Cidinha outside her long house in Brazil. It is made from earth on a wooden frame. Small windows keep it cool on hot days.

My house is by the football pitch.

Sara lives near the North Pole in Alaska, part of the United States of America. It is very snowy. Her house keeps her warm in the icy climate.

My dad has to shovel the snow to open the door.

Xin's front door leads right into the hillside! Her home has been carved from the rock. She lives in Shanaxi Province in China.

The walls of my house are very strong!

Victoria lives in a block of flats in London, the capital city of England in the United Kingdom. There are buzzers at the front of the building so families can open the door without leaving their homes.

I like playing in the gardens outside our flat.

This is Chanthong with her mum and her sister outside their house on stilts in Cambodia. The roof is made from palm leaves.

Even when it floods, our house on stilts stays dry.

Kari's family live in a tent covered with animal skins. Their reindeer give them meat to eat and milk to drink. They have settled in a national park near Khovsgol Lake in Mongolia.

Our tent is warm when the weather is cold.

This little building is one of the Bharmal family's rooms. There are more rooms further round the wall. The family lives in Rajasthan, India.

It only rains once or twice a year where we live.

Yanni and his family all live in a caravan that is pulled from place to place by their horses. Sometimes lots of Roma families travel together along the roads of Romania.

Our caravan is our home wherever we stop.

Malek, Bulbabur and Gasbano are from Pakistan. Their homes are made from tree branches bent over and covered in mud.

We live on a sand dune mountain.

Fatimata's camel waits patiently outside her house made of clay. She lives in a village in Mauritania with lots of other families.

My camel doesn't mind the hot sun but I like to stay cool.

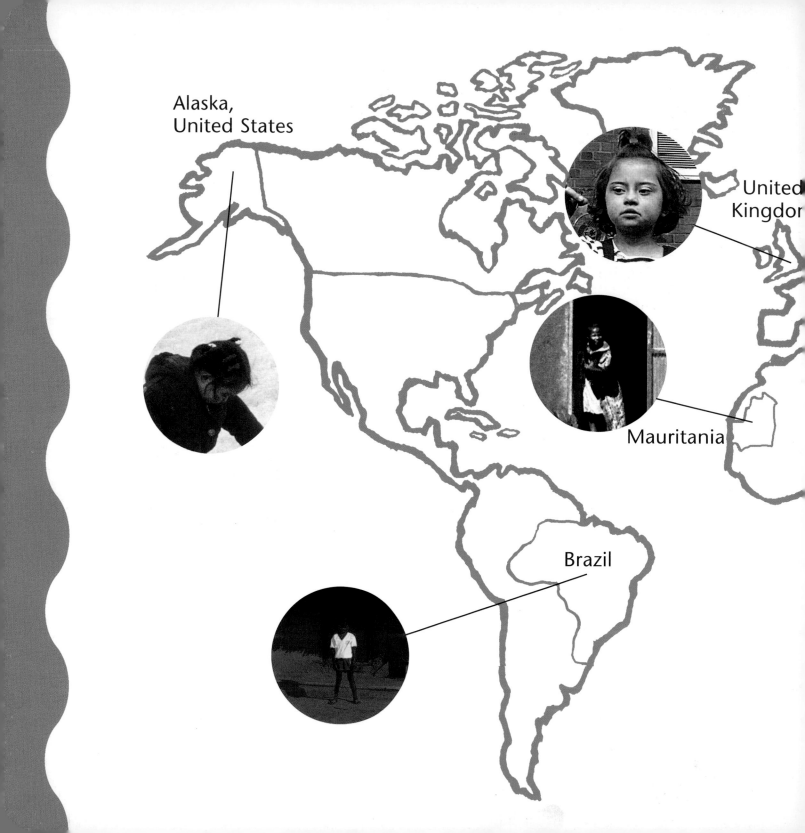

Alaska,
United States

United
Kingdom

Mauritania

Brazil

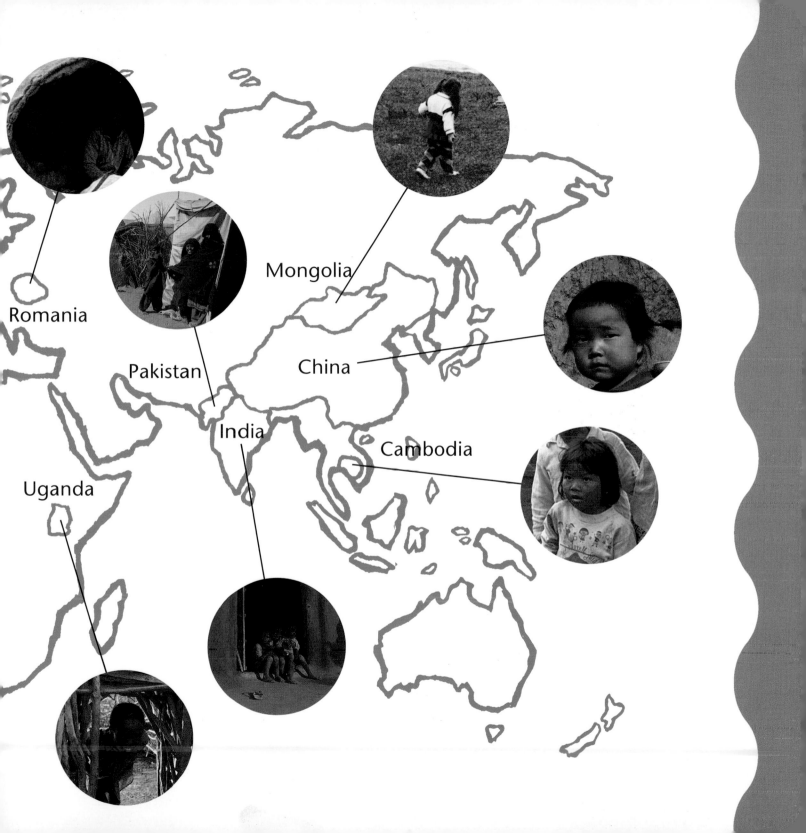

Romania

Mongolia

Pakistan

China

India

Cambodia

Uganda

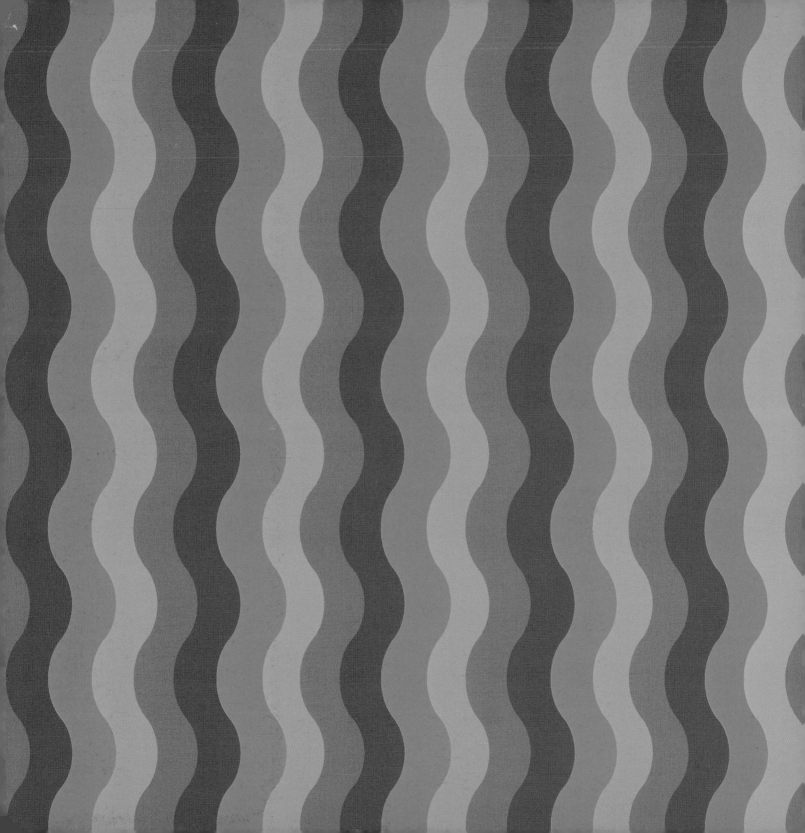

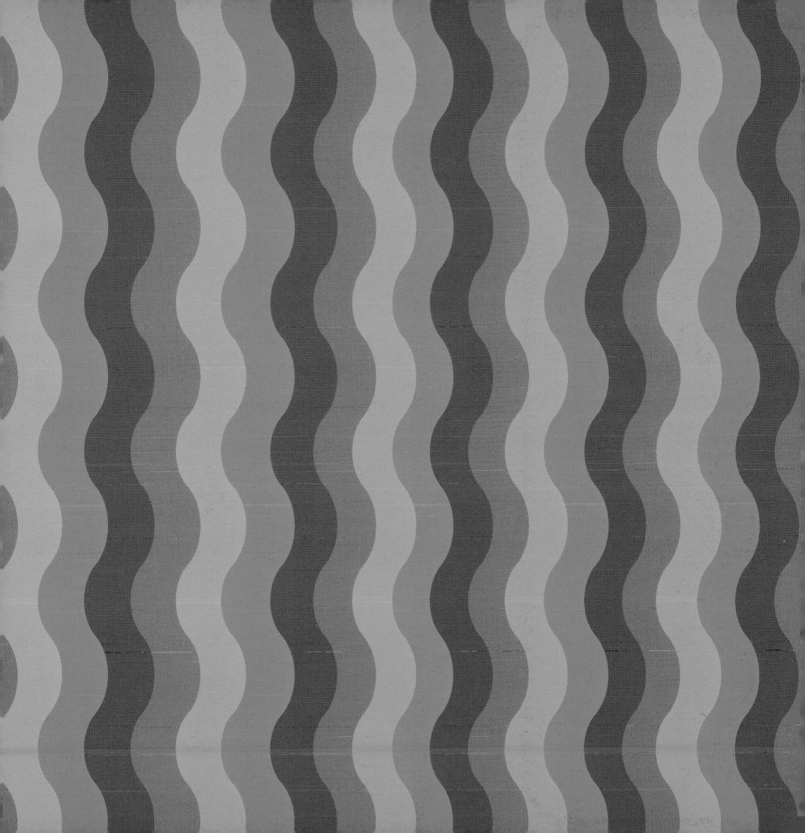

MORE BOOKS IN THE AROUND THE WORLD SERIES
FROM FRANCES LINCOLN

HAIR
Kate Petty
In association with Oxfam

We wear our hair in lots of different ways. Sometimes it is
to keep cool. Sometimes it is to look nice for a special occasion.
This book has photographs from all around the world
of some wonderful hairstyles.

ISBN: 978-1-84507-553-8

BICYCLES
Kate Petty
In association with Oxfam

There are all sorts of bicycles in the world.
Some people use them to get to school. Others use them
to play with their friends. This book has photographs of people
from all around the world using bicycles in lots of different ways.

ISBN: 978-1-84507-554-5

PLAYTIME
Kate Petty
In association with Oxfam

Every child enjoys playtime and has a favourite toy or game.
This book looks at photographs of children from all around the world
having fun playing alone or with their friends.

ISBN: 978-1-84507-555-2

Frances Lincoln titles are available from all good bookshops.
You can also buy books and find out more about your favourite titles,
authors and illustrators on our website: www.franceslincoln.com